Jeff Gordon

RACING'S DRIVING FORCE

BECKETT PUBLICATIONS

Jeff Gordon: Racing's Driving Force
Copyright ©2000 by Beckett Publications
All rights reserved under International and
Pan-American Copyright Conventions.
Printed in Canada

Published by: Beckett Publications
15850 Dallas Parkway
Dallas, Texas 75248

ISBN: 1-887432-85-X
Beckett® is a registered trademark of
Beckett Publications.

First Edition: April 2000
Beckett Corporate Sales and Information
(972) 991-6657

EDITORIAL CONTRIBUTORS

Jim McLaurin, who interviewed Ray
Evernham for the foreword, covers auto
racing for *The State* in Columbia, South
Carolina.

Monte Dutton, who interviewed Bobby
Allison for Chapter 1, Kenny Wallace for
Chapter 4, and Dale Earnhardt for Chapter
6, covers auto racing for the *Gaston Gazette*
in Gastonia, North Carolina.

Johnny D. Boggs, who wrote Chapters 2,
3 and 5, is a freelance writer based in
Santa Fe, New Mexico.

Richard Huff, who wrote Chapter 7, covers auto racing and media for the *New York
Daily News* and is an author of several racing books.

Tom Gillispie, who interviewed John
Hendrick for Chapter 8, is a freelance
writer based in Kernersville, North
Carolina.

PHOTO CREDITS

AP/Wide World Photos: 86, 106 (bottom),
   107
Courtesy of Action Performance Co.: 42 (top)
Courtesy of John & Carol Bickford: 34, 35,
   36, 37, 38, 40, 41, 49 (bottom), 50
   (bottom)
Chobat Racing Images: 6–7, 46, 57, 60, 69
   (bottom), 72
CIA Stock Photography: 123
Greg Crisp: 79
Scott Cunningham: 31
Butch Dill: 87
Tom DiPace: 84
Gary Eller/CIA Stock Photography: 121 (left)
Don Grassman/CIA Stock Photography: 65
   (bottom), 67, 74, 76, 78
Harold Hinson: 20, 21, 24, 25, 26, 52, 77, 91
   (top), 114, 124
Craig Jones/Allsport: 71
Nigel Kinrade: 2–3, 5, 8, 11, 12, 15 (bottom),
   16, 45, 49 (top), 51, 53, 55, 56, 58, 61, 64,
   65 (top), 66, 68, 70, 81, 82, 83, 85, 88, 91
   (bottom), 92–93, 94, 96, 97, 99, 101, 102,
   109, 110, 113, 116, 120
John Mahoney: 32, 39, 42 (bottom), 43
Tim Mantoani: cover
Ernest Masche: 50 (top)
Will & Deni McIntyre/Outline: 105, 106 (top)
Dozier Mobley: 63
Courtesy of National Fluid Milk Processor
   Promotion Board: 108
Joanna Nisbet/Phil Aull Studios: 75
Frank W. Ockenfels/Outline: 1
Courtesy of Outback Steakhouse: 48
Todd Rosenberg/Allsport: 15 (top)
Brian Spurlock: 18, 22–23, 28, 44, 80, 90,
   95, 98, 104, 112, 118, 119, 121 (right),
   122, 123
Gene Sweeney: 30
David Taylor/Allsport: 69 (top)
George Tiedemann/Sports Illustrated: 62
Paul Webb: 27

Contents

FOREWORD

I remember the first time I ever saw Jeff Gordon. It was at a hotel in Charlotte in 1990. We were going to work together on a Busch Grand National test. We met in the lobby to cover some notes for the next day.

He was just a kid. He had long hair and a little moustache. He had a briefcase; I had a briefcase. I open up my briefcase to take out some notes. He opens up his and he's got a jar of peanuts, a Nintendo Game Boy and a stock car racing magazine in there. He takes out his pad and pen, and he calls me Mr. Evernham for about an hour.

By Ray Evernham
As Told To Jim McLaurin

I had seen him drive on TV and I knew he was pretty sharp, because I used to watch a lot of the ESPN *Thunder* stuff. But I thought, "We'll see if he's just TV hype or if he can really do it."

He was just an awfully nice young man, and he seemed awfully savvy about a race car.

The next day, we went to Charlotte Motor Speedway. We put Chuck Bown in the car to shake it down, and then we put Jeff in. Jeff went out immediately and ran as fast, if not faster, than Chuck had been running.

He turned it tremendously sideways coming off of turn four, sort of got in the bumps and went dead sideways. He corrected that thing and put it on the straightaway and never bobbled it. It never over-corrected. It was like he was in a sprint car.

We all looked at one another and said, "This boy is pretty good."

In those first days, it was just fun. He was very naive about the cars, and NASCAR in general. In the Busch series, he didn't have a lot of pressure on him. We used to travel back and forth to the races in his car.

There was a time we shared a hotel room. That's the way we traveled in those days. As we grew into Winston Cup, it grew more hectic, and, of course, we grew apart as it went.

But in the beginning, it was just two guys making a living in a Busch car.

I think Jeff would have been successful anytime; I think (car owner) Rick Hendrick would have been successful anytime; I think I would have been successful any-time, but I don't think that we could

Jeff didn't look the part of distinguished veteran driver when he met Ray, but the teen-ager with the toy-filled briefcase was all business.

Evernham's knowledge and steadying influence helped mold Gordon into auto racing's preeminent talent. The two combined for three Winston Cup championships and forty-seven Cup victories as part of the Hendrick Motorsports team before parting ways midway through the 1999 season.

have achieved what we achieved without one another. What we did was pretty special.

Was John Elway a great quarterback? Sure, but for years he didn't have the right people to show how great he was. Certainly we would have all done well, but in the situation we were in, we were able to become championship material.

As he was standing in victory lane (in Charlotte in October, 1999, two weeks after Evernham left the team) or the week before, he said he wouldn't have been there without me.

I really feel like I wouldn't be sitting here right now with this

Dodge program without him and the Rainbow Warriors. We're a big part of each other's success.

He gets a chance to prove himself as more than just a hired gun, and I get a chance to prove myself as a businessperson and team owner. You can't discount Rick Hendrick's input and the Rainbow Warriors, but we helped each other get to the next stage of our lives. It's unfortunate that it wasn't together, but we still are where we want to be.

If there's a dark side to Jeff, I've never seen that side of him. He's a good kid. As you go through life, not everybody's gonna be happy with you. I think from where he's started to where he's at now, and how he's represented the sport, he's done a tremendous job.

You look: He was twenty-one years old and a superstar. You compare him to some football and basketball players — compare him to

Mike Tyson — and look at the difference.

Here's a young Christian man who loves his wife. He takes criticism because she's in the limelight a lot. My God! Let's hate the guy: He's a great race car driver, he's a good young Christian and he loves his wife? What's there to hate?

He never has been in the normal mold, not even as a sprint car driver. People say he's not your typical "NASCAR driver," but he wasn't an outlaw-type sprint car driver, either. He's just an extremely talented young man who tries to protect his personal life.

You're gonna have bumpy roads with everybody, even with people as close as your family, but I can honestly tell you that I respect him for the person he is because he's not a hypocrite.

He's sincere about what he believes in, and he walks the talk. Not a lot of people do that.

That's something that, being in your twenties and being a millionaire, isn't easy to do, especially with the amount of press coverage and things that he could get himself into that a lot of other young sports people get into.

A lot of people don't know how to read it, because he's protective of his personal life — as he should be — but they don't know and understand a lot of things he does do for people.

Is he the best driver I've ever seen? I've said it over and over. To me, Jeff Gordon's the best person to ever hold a steering wheel.

He's got all the aspects: He's a thinker, he's a doer, he's got the talent to drive a car. He's got great car control, great stamina, and he's got the perfect size. He can do all the media stuff. He's got everything.

When you go down that check box, he's got all the checks.

I honestly don't know what his

Evernham says Jeff doesn't fit the stereotype of the typical young super-star athlete: spoiled, immature and of the belief that he or she is above the law. In other words, Gordon is no Mike Tyson.

legacy will be. I've said it a lot of times: That's gonna be up to him. He's the one who's gonna control that.

He's gonna win as much as he wants to, and when he feels like it's time to do something else, he'll do it.

He can continue to re-write the record books. There's no stopping him. He did it in quarter-midgets and midgets, he did it in sprint cars, and we were well on our way to doing that in a Busch program and stopped to go to Winston Cup. Then he did it in Winston Cup.

He's got the key. I sometimes had to push him to tell him that, and I've been telling him for years that he just didn't need me, that he could do it on his own.

Now that he knows that, there's gonna be no stopping him.

*When Jeff Gordon and **Ray Evernham** split up the most successful team in Winston Cup racing in 1999, many in the NASCAR community didn't know what to think.*

But some fans — and insiders — were expecting Gordon to fall flat on his face. Since the two had been together as driver and crew chief from Gordon's first day in a stock car, many couldn't believe Gordon was talented enough to win three Winston Cup championships on his own.

But Gordon went out the very next weekend and won his first race without the highly respected Evernham pulling the strings. Then, to prove it wasn't a fluke, he and new crew chief Brian Whitesell did it again one week later. Least surprised by Jeff's success was his old friend Ray.

"Shucks," Evernham said. "I knew it all along."

"I've said it over and over. To me, Jeff Gordon's the best person to ever hold a steering wheel," says Evernham.

THE RAINBOW WARRIOR

David Pearson used to be the smartest driver ever. Note that I say "used to be." When I was competing in the NASCAR Winston Cup Series, I never thought I would see a driver smarter than Pearson. But I have.

Pearson used his head. He never forgot that the main mission was getting the checkered flag at the end of the race. Pearson knew how to take care of the car. He knew how to address situations in traffic. He had a knack for timing it so that he would come up on the lapped cars at just the right time, where they would be easiest to pass.

By Bobby Allison
As Told To Monte Dutton

David Pearson didn't just outrun his opponents; he outwitted them. That's how the three-time Winston Cup champion — and ten-time winner at the treacherous Darlington Raceway — earned the nickname "Sly Fox," amended to "Silver Fox" during Pearson's gray-headed years.

Some of the things Pearson did seem simple talking about them now, but on the racetrack, they were remarkable. The thing that made Pearson so great was that he could relax in a race car. I don't believe he was any more excited than if he'd been walking down the street. He never let his emotions get the best of him.

And Jeff Gordon is smarter than Pearson ever was.

Gordon's success proves you can still win races by outsmarting people and by using strategy. A lot of drivers today don't believe this. They say: "Back in the old days, you could hang back and bide your time and come to the front when the time came. Now the sport is so competitive that you can't do that. You have to drive every lap as hard as you possibly can."

Yet Gordon uses strategy just like Pearson did. You see him bide his time, save his car and move to the front when the time comes. Now, certainly, the competition is closer than it ever was, but that's a product of the game, of technology advancing over time and the fact that equipment is more durable and reliable nowadays.

No matter how good your equipment is, though, you've still got to be able to do the driving, and Gordon is very, very good at that.

I think I see in Gordon things that he seldom gets credit for. I see the personal commitment of a champion. He does his job and puts up with whatever conditions exist on that day. If his foot was getting

Gordon's success is proof drivers can still win by outsmarting the competition, Allison says. "You see him bide his time, save his car and move to the front when the time comes."

"Road course, big track, little track:
He's the man to beat at all of them,"
Allison says.

Since entering Winston Cup competition full-time in 1993, Jeff has been backed by a first-rate crew. And thanks to Gordon's talent and toughness, Evernham and Co. have been able to take chances other crews wouldn't dream of taking.

blistered, he'd go right on and let his foot get blistered. A lot of guys, if their foot was getting blistered, they'd pull right into the pits and ask for relief.

Here's another testament to Gordon's greatness: He does what it takes, and he never gives up.

Something you see all the time is when a yellow flag comes out and everybody else pits, but he stays out. Or everybody else changes four tires and Gordon's crew just changes two. In other words, they put him at a disadvantage, but then he wins anyway. That's the mark of a great driver. He does the best he can with what he's got, and more times than not, that's good enough to win.

Having a driver like that also gives the crew chief options. If

you've got Jeff Gordon driving for you, you can take a chance. Gordon's talent more than makes up for the disadvantage. With Gordon behind the wheel, you take track position every time, but if there's any way to hold on, he'll do it. Gordon accepts whatever he's got and makes the best of it.

Looks are deceiving with Gordon. He's a little guy, and it's easy to sell him short because he's so neat and polite. There's never a hair out of place, but it's pretty

Rick Hendrick provided the first-rate equipment. Ray Evernham provided the guidance to help Gordon reach his full potential.

obvious, isn't it? This kid's no pretty boy.

Look at the tracks. Which ones are the toughest? Darlington, Bristol, Dover, Martinsville . . . it doesn't matter. The tougher the track, the likelier it is that Gordon will win. That, too, is the mark of a great driver. Road course, big track, little track: He's the man to beat at all of them.

Another thing that Gordon had going for him in the early years of his career was Ray Evernham. I like Ray a lot. I don't know why they've split up, but more power to him.

He did a really nice job for Gordon. As good as he is, Jeff couldn't have won on a bicycle. He had to have a decent car, so I've got nothing but admiration for both of them.

Gordon really does use strategy and drive the car great, but Evernham did a really nice job of preparation and communication. He gave a great young driver the information and encouragement that enabled him to fulfill his potential.

Two times in my career, I had a person like that on the other end. I had the first radio, and early on, I had Ralph Moody in the pits on the radio. That was in my second go-around with Holman-Moody, in 1971.

I would say, "Oh, the car's impossible to drive," and Ralph would just say, "Don't worry, we'll fix it." I won nine out of nineteen starts. And then I had Gary Nelson, and I'd say, "Gary, this car's awful. It's sliding," and he'd say, "Don't worry, we'll fix it."

If they're going to fix it, all I've got to do is drive. I only had to worry about my end of the equation. That's the importance of having a great crew chief. I always felt like I could devote one hundred percent of my attention to my job if my job was driving.

If my job was being the car owner and the bill payer and the director of maintenance and the director of chassis setup — and driver — then I couldn't put one hundred percent into driving. But I won races when I didn't have that perfect situation, and if Gordon ever gets in that situation, he will, too.

In fact my opinion of Gordon, as far as the driving goes, is that he is the second best ever. Who was the best? Well, let me put it to you this way. There's a guy who has won eighty-five times but only gets credit for eighty-four of them right now. He won races in nine different brands of cars for fourteen different race teams. That guy probably was the best driver.

Not so surprisingly, the driver with eighty-five victories who only gets credit for eighty-four sounds a lot like . . . **Bobby Allison**. *Allison won a Grand National race at Bowman Gray Stadium in Winston-Salem, North Carolina, driving a Ford Mustang. At that time, NASCAR was struggling to come up with enough cars to fill its fields, so the governing body allowed cars from the old "baby grands" (Grand American) division to compete. But because Allison won the race in a car that was not Grand National, he was never given credit in the all-time standings.*

Gordon still needs quite a few victories to catch Bobby Allison. The Hall of Fame driver and patriarch of the legendary Allison racing family claimed eighty-four wins during his **NASCAR** racing career.

STARTING LINE

Jeff Gordon earned the nickname Wonder Boy for his dominance on the NASCAR circuit while still in his early twenties. Truthfully, Gordon was a veteran winner before he first climbed into a NASCAR Busch or Winston Cup series car. He had been out-racing the competition since kindergarten.

Gordon was born on August 4, 1971, in Vallejo, California, the son of Will and Carol Gordon. His parents divorced when Jeff was just an infant, and Jeff lived with his mother and older sister, Kim. In 1972, Carol began dating John

By Johnny D. Boggs

Right: Jeff and his sister, Kim, tagged along on John and Carol's first date to the races at Vallejo Speedway. Not long after Jeff was hooked.
Below: Jeff speeds up the street in front of his house on a new BMX bike. "I used to ride my bike, skateboard, roller skates – whatever I had," Jeff says.

tant role in coaching and steering the young boy toward victory lane.

Jeff showed an early interest in speed. He was a child in perpetual motion, always racing on his bicycle, skateboard or roller skates

Bickford, and the two married three years later.

The stepfather, whose first date with Carol was an outing to the races at Vallejo Speedway with Jeff and Kim, would play an impor-

Jeff at age two, before he took to gripping a steering wheel instead of a football.

Above: Jeff at four while on a camping trip with his family.
Right: Jeff gets an earful at his fourth birthday party.

throughout the neighborhood. So it seemed only natural that Bickford bought the four-year-old a quarter-midget, 2.85-horsepower racer. No one could predict then how naturally Gordon would take to the wheels.

"We went out and made a racetrack out of the local fairgrounds there in Vallejo," Bickford says. "He and I would go out every chance I could get away from work. We'd run hundreds of laps. The motor would get so hot it wouldn't run."

After practicing under the supervision of Bickford for about a year, Jeff began competing in quarter-midget races in the area. He was

Jeff, at age seven, poses with his trophy won in a quarter-midget race at Baylands Track in California.

five years old. Three years later, Jeff won his first of three quarter-midget national championships. He kept winning, too, sometimes beating drivers seventeen or older. Some parents started complaining, accusing Jeff of being a midget or lying about his age.

When he was nine, Jeff began racing ten-horsepower go-karts. He entered twenty-five races around the Vallejo area and won them all. He captured four class championships in go-kart competition before making the leap to seven-hundred-horsepower sprint cars at age fourteen.

"I wasn't so sure about what we were doing," Gordon says. "It wasn't normal because there weren't any other people my age. Then, after all that nervousness about starting the car (sprint cars must be push started), I got that down pretty good. Then, it was going to a race.

It was like starting all over again with that quarter-midget. Here I am, doing something I don't know anything about. I was pretty nervous. Then, once I got a few laps, it started becoming natural."

By then, Jeff's parents realized their prodigy had a real future in professional auto racing. They also understood that they had run out of races in California. Age restrictions in California prevented Jeff — who was too young to even have a driver's license — from competing against adults.

The family looked east to Indiana, home to the famed Indianapolis 500 and no racing age restrictions. So they packed up and moved to Pittsboro, a small town of about one thousand near Indianapolis, and, with his parents' permission, Jeff started racing on the new circuit.

New state. New tracks.

New competition. Same results.

Between 1985 and 1988 Jeff won twenty-two races, claimed twenty-one pole positions and finished in the top five fifty-five times. When he was sixteen, he became

Jeff's racing education included a visit to the Indianapolis Motor Speedway Museum in 1983.

Jeff in his sprint-car racing suit at age
fifteen, and driving a quarter-midget
car.

Jeff claimed his first USAC victory at a sprint race in Florence, Kentucky, on May 20, 1989.

the youngest driver to earn a racing license from the United States Auto Club. Meanwhile, he attended Tri-West High School, a small school with an enrollment of about 350 in four grades. All the while he kept on racing and winning.

But Jeff remained a typical high school kid. In fact, he was a model student: clean-cut, conscientious, polite — the All-American boy. "What he is now is what he was then," says Jim Coon, who taught math and coached basketball while Jeff attended Tri-West.

Early on, few classmates knew what the modest new kid was all about. Once school was out on Friday, Jeff's mother or stepfather, or maybe a family friend, would pick him up, and they'd be off to the races somewhere in central Indiana or into Illinois. Then Jeff would come back home, and on

Monday, he would be sitting in class.

When he wasn't racing, though, he could often be found cheering on the Tri-West Bruins. Recalls Coon: "I remember when I was basketball coach and on Friday night, if he wasn't racing, he would be on the front row of the student section cheering on his classmates and holding up signs, just being a high school fan. And he did the same thing during football season.

Jeff's teachers say he wasn't much different than other students at Pittsboro's Tri-West High: polite, supportive and hard-working. "What he is now is what he was then," says teacher Jim Coon.

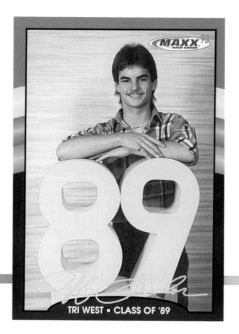

Jeff's sprint-car career took him to many locales, from Eldora Speedway (right) to New Zealand's Western Springs Track (left) to the World Sprint Car Championship in Australia (below). "People don't know how many times Jeff Gordon slept in pickup trucks and worked his [butt] off, fixing the cars himself," Bickford says.

He wasn't a player, but when he could be there, he and his buddies were the rowdies in the crowd. They had a good time. And that was what high school sports were supposed to be about."

It wasn't until late in his junior year that Jeff developed a certain celebrity status at Tri-West. The sports cable television network ESPN began broadcasting *Thursday Night Thunder* at the .686-mile Indianapolis Raceway Park, just a few miles from Tri-West where Jeff often raced. "All of a sudden somebody would say, 'Hey, I'm in class with him and he's racing on TV,' " Coon says.

Some classmates started following Jeff's career. He often would be congratulated on a victory in the halls, or friends would wish him luck before a race. But the attention given him was no more

Right: Bickford committed to Jeff's racing from the start. "We had the whole system that everybody dreams of having in the professional ranks, and we were doing it in amateur racing," Bickford says. "It was very, very organized. We put in a tremendous amount of effort — he and I and his mother."

Below: Gordon once won two races in one day at Salem Speedway.

than students would give an athlete on one of the school's team sports before or after a big game.

"At no time did he try to take advantage (of his notoriety), and he probably could have — especially his junior and senior years — if his family would have wanted to," Coon says.

Still, sometimes Jeff would have to leave school early or get back late because of a weekend racing engagement. But it wasn't like he was playing hooky or cutting classes to turn a few laps on some Midwest oval.

Not long before Jeff made the switch to stock cars, Gordon claimed the USAC Silver Crown "Hulman Hundred" at the Indiana State Fairgrounds in Indianapolis on May 24, 1991.

"He was very conscientious about getting his work turned in on time, making sure everything was on the up-and-up and was just a very polite young student," Coon says. "And I think that's a direct credit to his upbringing. John and Carol just did a great job making sure he did the right thing."

Jeff graduated from Tri-West in 1989 — entering a race the night of his graduation — and began racing full time. Gordon entered sprint car races in Australia and New Zealand, became the 1989 USAC midget rookie of the year and won the USAC midget championship in 1990 and the USAC Silver Crown in 1991.

"I think anybody who watched Jeff race when he was still in high school saw that he had a unique talent," says Coon, now the assistant principal and athletic director at Tri-West. "He has that innate ability that a lot of them don't have, and that's to drive out on the edge without being dangerous. But I don't think anybody could have predicted (all he would accomplish)."

It was time to move up again. But where? Indiana was the birthplace of Indy-car racing in the United States, a sport where Mario Andretti, Johnny Rutherford and A.J. Foyt had captured trophies, admiration and truckloads of money. But then there was the National Association for Stock Car Auto Racing, which was booming.

After his 1990 midget championship, John Bickford suggested that Jeff attend the Buck Baker driving school in Rockingham, North Carolina. During his career

Before he was king of Winston Cup racing, he was the pride of Pittsboro, Indiana, a small town outside Indianapolis where Jeff learned many of the values he still reflects today.

in what became the NASCAR Winston Cup series, Buck Baker won forty-six races and the 1956 and '57 championships.

Jeff was just nineteen years old, with some five hundred racing victories, when he sat behind the wheel of his first NASCAR stock car. It took only a couple of laps

Three Winston Cup championships later, Gordon remains driven to succeed.

around North Carolina Motor Speedway's 1.017-mile oval for Jeff to realize he wanted to make NASCAR his career.

Bill Davis would give him that chance.

PIT STOP

Jeff Gordon remained on the USAC circuit in 1991, but the lingering buzz from his stock car spin had convinced him to leave open-wheel racing behind.

The next step: convincing car owner Bill Davis he was worthy of a NASCAR Busch Grand National ride. Davis, a former motorcycle racer and Mark Martin's Winston Cup gas man in 1982, had scored three Busch victories between 1988 and 1990 with Martin behind the wheel. But now Davis needed a replacement for Martin. He took a gamble that Gordon could parlay what he had

By Johnny D. Boggs

Jeff made the transition from sprint cars to the Busch series late in the 1990 season, initially driving a Ford sponsored by Outback Steakhouse.

learned on the USAC circuits to the NASCAR series.

Gordon would soon be paired with a crew chief fourteen years his senior. They seemed an unlikely team, but New Jersey native Ray Evernham and the young, mustachioed Gordon would become fast friends.

The chemistry between the two — Evernham served as a friend and father, coach and mentor, big brother and, later, best man at Gordon's wedding — was perfect.

"He was a steadying influence on a young and highly talented driver," Bob Latford, a longtime NASCAR official and editor of *The Inside Line Newsletter*, says of Evernham. "He was able to control the emotions and bursts of energy, because when (Gordon) came in he hadn't run long races, and it takes a whole different approach to run two-hundred-lappers than it does to run fifty-lappers."

In August, Gordon drove his Thunderbird (that's right; the future Winston Cup champion long associated with his brightly painted

Chevrolets steered a Ford during his first two years on the Busch circuit) to the pole position at Orange County Speedway in Rougemont, North Carolina.

"What impressed me more than his performance was the kid's infectious personality," says Winkie Wilkins, then the general manager at the .375-mile speedway. "He never met a stranger, never met anyone, he didn't wind up being comfortable with, including me."

Some businessmen in the area took such a liking to Gordon that they helped his team buy race-day

Left: After pairing with Mark Martin for some modest Busch series success, Bill Davis went looking for a new driver for the 1991 season. Knowing talent when he saw it, Davis quickly signed Gordon.

Below: Gordon drove the No. 1 Carolina Ford Dealers car during his first full Busch campaign, scoring five top-five finishes.

Above: Jeff took home $111,608 in winnings in 1991 — and Busch rookie of the year honors.
Below: Sponsorship for Jeff's 1992 Busch season shifted to Baby Ruth — fitting considering Jeff's age relative to his racing peers at the time.

tires or other forms of sponsorship, or even gave him a plane ride to another event.

"There are people here now who are fans of his because they simply saw him grow up," Wilkins says. "He won over a lot of people."

Gordon had that effect everywhere he went.

Jim Hunter, president of Darlington Raceway, recalls his first impressions of the young driver: "It's not how hard you go into the corners here, it's how soon you can

get back in the throttle to get back out of the corner. Jeff Gordon was as smooth a rookie as I've ever seen run this place, and he probably didn't have what by today's standards we would call a smooth-handling car."

Yet one of Hunter's fondest memories of Gordon came not on the racetrack, but on a golf course. Gordon was teamed with Hunter, racing official T. Wayne Robertson and South Carolina Governor David Beasley in a celebrity event. Unlike NASCAR driver Dale Jarrett, Gordon is far from a scratch golfer, and as Hunter notes, "No athlete likes to go get on somebody else's turf and perform."

Hunter was impressed with Gordon's hand-eye coordination, and the young driver connected on some good shots. That impressed Hunter even more, especially when Gordon started talking about having been paired once with golf leg-

The veteran competition on the Busch circuit prepared Gordon well for his ascent to the Winston Cup circuit in 1993.

end Arnold Palmer and what a thrill that had been. Eventually, Hunter asked Gordon how often he played golf. He was shocked when Gordon said this was probably only the third time he had ever played the game.

Good hand-eye coordination is also a must in NASCAR competition, and Gordon put his to good use, improving with each race and learning all he could from Evernham — and his own mistakes.

"Jeff Gordon was as smooth a rookie as I've ever seen run this place, and he probably didn't have what by today's standards we would call a smooth-handling car." — Jim Hunter, president of Darlington Raceway

He scored five top-five and ten top-ten finishes in his rookie season on the Busch circuit and took home $111,608 in winnings. Better yet, he finished eleventh in the points race and earned rookie of the year honors.

In 1992, Gordon again found himself behind the wheel of Bill Davis's Busch car, this time a Baby Ruth-sponsored T-Bird. He started off strong, winning poles at Rockingham and Richmond. On

March 14, he landed the Atlanta 300 pole, the first Busch race ever held at the 1.5-mile Atlanta Motor Speedway. Atlanta was a fast super-speedway that had held Winston Cup races since 1960.

Gordon's qualifying speed had been a whopping 173.821 mph, and he was competing against several regular Cup drivers. Gordon drove strong that Saturday afternoon, and one influential man watching the race took an interest in the young driver. Rick Hendrick, who owned the Winston Cup cars driven by Ken Schrader and Ricky Rudd, wanted to field a three-car team for 1993. When Gordon went on to win at Atlanta for his first NASCAR victory, Hendrick took mental notes.

"I was impressed with how he could drive so fast and so out of control," Hendrick said later. "I've never seen anyone remind me of (the late Tim Richmond) the way he did."

Gordon continued to improve. In May, he scored another pole at Charlotte and earned his second victory. The next month Jeff claimed the pole position at Myrtle Beach, South Carolina, with a speed of 198.595 mph — a record that stood for five years. In October, Gordon returned to Charlotte to win another pole and score his third win of the season.

In all, Gordon posted a record eleven poles with ten top-fives and fifteen top tens. His winnings reached $412,293, and he finished fourth in the points race to eventual Winston Cup drivers Joe Nemechek, Bobby Labonte and Todd Bodine.

Gordon had done everything NASCAR asked him to do to promote the Busch series. The Busch series was great, too, but it is to the Winston Cup what Triple-A baseball is to the major leagues. The Winston Cup . . . now that was the show. And Jeff Gordon wanted to drive on the Winston Cup circuit.

People had taken notice. Davis was forming a Cup team, but he struggled to find proper sponsorship. Cale Yarborough expressed an interest, too, but in the end it was Hendrick who signed Gordon to his first Winston Cup contract. Seven celebratory years later, Hendrick would re-sign Gordon to a lifetime deal.

Hendrick remembered watching Gordon race to victory at Atlanta back in March. He knew the kid could drive, but he also saw something else. So did Darlington's Hunter. "He is a good-looking young guy, number one," Hunter says. "He's very articulate in his mannerisms. He's very upbeat in talking about racing. . . . It's almost like he's living a fairy tale. The best

Jeff visited victory lane three times in 1992, winning twice at Charlotte and once at Atlanta.

NASCAR Winston Cup Series
HARLOTTE MOTOR SPEEDWAY
CHAMPION 30
Wins
Baby Ruth
Ford
1

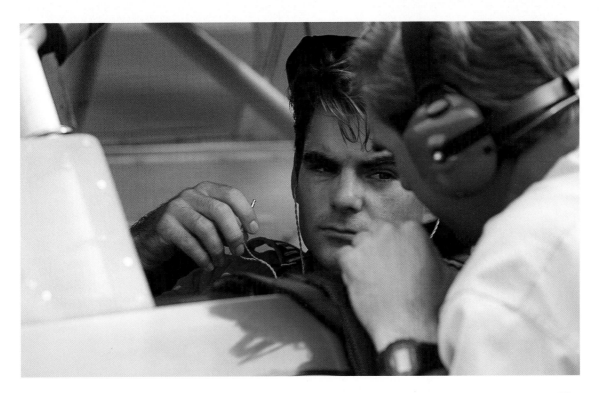

thing I can say about Jeff off the track, and from a sponsor's point of view, is that Jeff understands what drives the sport from a money standpoint and appreciates sponsors and the role sponsors play."

So Gordon and Evernham left for Charlotte, Davis hired Bobby Labonte as the driver of his Cup team for 1993 and Yarborough settled for Derrike Cope.

Gordon ran his first NASCAR Winston Cup race in the Hooters 500 at Atlanta, the final race of the season. Rick Mast won the pole, Bill Elliott took the checkered flag, and

Perhaps the biggest dividend from Jeff's two-plus years on the Busch circuit was the relationship he cultivated with crew chief Ray Evernham.

Alan Kulwicki claimed the Cup championship. Gordon made a rookie mistake, wrecked early and did not finish his first race.

The Hooters 500 was also the final race of NASCAR legend Richard Petty. The "King" had garnered a record two hundred career victories, but he was moving out of the driver's seat for a full-time spot in the team owner's chair.

No one knew it at the time, but the torch had been passed in NASCAR Winston Cup competition.

"From the first time we all laid eyes on Gordon, we all knew he was a rare talent."
— Kenny Wallace

CLOSING THE GAP

Let me tell you something about Jeff Gordon. Jeff is an all-American boy who is a damn good driver — gifted from God when he was born.

When I raced Jeff in the Busch series, Jeff was wearing Reebok tennis shoes, jeans, sweat shirts, T-shirts. Jeff today is still a great person. The only thing that has changed about Jeff, out of everything, is that he married a model, and she straightened him out. She got his old, scraggly moustache shaved off.

Brooke Gordon is a great lady who has showed Jeff the world: fine clothes, religion . . .

By Kenny Wallace
As Told To Monte Dutton

Jeff proved to be the cream of a strong 1993 Winston Cup rookie crop that included Kenny Wallace (right) and Bobby Labonte (center).

It is truly Brooke who has changed Jeff, and that is not at all a bad thing. But, when it's just me and Jeff, one-on-one, he's still the same "Jeff Gord" from 1991.

When I came from St. Louis, came down south to race stock cars, my brother Rusty told me, "Herm, I'm not going to feed you to the wolves. I'm going to teach you the ropes in this sport, and then I'm going to let you go like a little bird."

Now, with Gordon, maybe it wasn't planned this way, but it's the way it's worked out. Ray Evernham gave Jeff a calming effect, a confidence, and a conviction that everything the two of them did together was going to be right.

The kid's got forty-something wins, three championships, and now kind of knows it all on his own. Now Ray can let Jeff go like a little bird.

There's something we all know about, but we don't talk about. I think the biggest example of that is (crew chief) Todd Parrott and Dale Jarrett. I believe it was D.J. who almost got fired out of the 28 car because Ernie Irvan was coming back from injury.

There was a moment when D.J. was in limbo. Then, all of a sudden, this guy who's forty or forty-one years old finds himself in the right situation and blossoms into an overnight superstar. He and Parrott were the match. They found each other, luckily, and the rest is history.

It's the same with Gordon. There's no doubt about Jeff's ability. We all know he's good. No, he's not good, he's great. We all know he's going to continue to win races. We

Wallace and Gordon battled head-to-head in the Hanes 500 in 1993. Gordon placed eighth, securing one of eleven rookie top-ten finishes.

Jeff's still the same polite, down-to-earth, competitive person he was when he crashed the Winston Cup scene in 1993, Wallace says, but wife Brooke (shown smooching Jeff after the 1994 Ray Brickyard) has helped make his life even better.

don't even want Jeff to prove us wrong. Jeff will finish out the end of this era still running good, because he's running what Ray built up.

Now Brian Whitesell, who is another person who has been

Jeff and Miss Winston Brooke Sealy already knew each other when he accepted the trophy for this Daytona qualifying race in 1993, and within days they were dating. By year's end, their private relationship had gone public.

tutored by Evernham, has to see if he can work with Jeff to carry on building new cars and starting from scratch. The only story is going to be: Can they get over it (Evernham's departure)? I think they will, no problem.

But aside from that, let's go back to the first time any of us became aware of Jeff Gordon. Some of us had seen this young guy running sprint cars, but we didn't really know what he was going to do when he showed up in the Busch Series.

Here was a seventeen-year-old kid coming in and already realizing how important taking care of equipment was. Now that may not sound as impressive as it really is, but that

is a truly rare gift for a young driver.

John Bickford, Jeff's stepfather, has told everybody word-for-word, that if a driver wants to be good, you don't put him in lousy equipment, because he won't know what good equipment is. He'll be all over the track, just driving it hard. Jeff had Mr. Bickford, who understood equipment, and when you mix good equipment with a great race driver, the result is Jeff Gordon.

Dale Earnhardt didn't seem to mind showing Jeff the ropes. The two spent much of their Speedweeks practice time at Daytona International Speedway drafting together.

Gordon followed up on his rookie of the year effort with a breakthrough 1994 campaign, which included victories in the Winston Select and Busch Clash — and taking the checkered flag in the inaugural Brickyard 400.

Gordon was smart enough to realize that when he came into the Busch Grand National series. You see, when he drove the No. 1 Carolina Ford car, he ran like crap. I know he did, and everybody else knows he did.

But when he hired Evernham, that's when he became the Jeff Gordon that most everyone in America, maybe even the world, knows about now. There's something to be learned by all of us, because we saw a kid who really went for it.

Contrast Jeff's career, how he

was a sensation right from the out-
set, with Kenny Irwin's career.
Kenny's going to be the next Jeff
Gordon, right? He goes in the 28
car, and nothing against the people
there, but Irwin's got no mentor.
He's got no Ray Evernham. Irwin
was a sitting duck, period.

People just assumed that if
Irwin gets the 28 car, it's just going
to run good. That's just a bunch of
bull. He's supposed to run good in
that car because Davey Allison ran

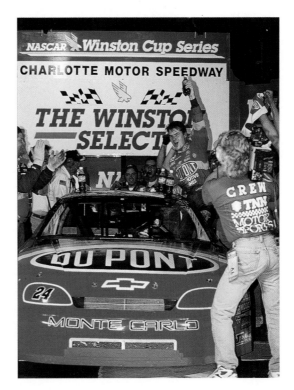

good, but when Davey was there, he had Jake Elder, he had Larry McReynolds, he had some of the greatest crew chiefs in the business. The (Harry) Melling car doesn't win now, and it's not just because Bill Elliott isn't in it anymore. It's a lot more complicated than people think, and it's about chemistry and teamwork and putting the right people together.

They need to repaint that damn 28 car. It's got a great identity, but give the guy driving it a break. Paint the car a different color; let it be just another race car.

I think Robert Yates, and Texaco, and maybe Ford Motor Company, got caught up in the whole "go find the next Jeff Gordon" thing. They all watched Jeff blossom into a superstar, but they learned the wrong lessons.

Now I think we've learned a lot of lessons from the Gordon story. The fans in the grandstands

Wallace says Gordon has been blessed with the best equipment, but it takes more than a great car to win on the Winston Cup circuit. Case in point: Kenny Irwin and the Texaco No. 28, once driven by Dale Jarrett.

Fans, according to Wallace, are seeing the product of God-given talent nurtured by a strong support network.

are knowledgeable, but they don't understand how things work down here. Their attitude is, "Is it the driver or is it the car? Give me an answer!"

They want it simple, but it's not simple.

So from the first time we all laid eyes on Gordon, we all knew he was a rare talent. But what separated Jeff from other talented drivers was that he combined all that God-given talent with the people around him: his wife, his stepfather, Ray Evernham — and there are others — who gave him the proper instruction on how to drive, how to manage his business affairs and how to live life to its fullest.

I think it's great. I have all the admiration in the world for Jeff and

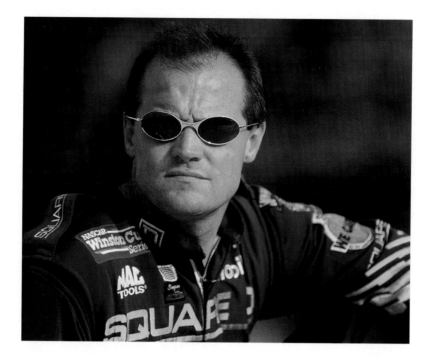

Despite finishing a respectable twenty-first in the Winston Cup standings in 1999, Wallace still awaits his turn in victory lane.

all the incredible things he's managed to accomplish in such a short time.

Kenny Wallace understands the value of teamwork in NASCAR Winston Cup competition. With brother Rusty providing guidance and support, Kenny finished third in Winston Cup rookie of the year balloting in 1993, two spots behind Gordon.

But Kenny and Jeff's careers took different paths following their rookie runs. Despite a successful stint with Robert Yates as Ernie Irvan's replacement for the final ten races of 1994, Wallace struggled to put together the winning combination during a three-year run with FILMAR Racing.

Now that he's a member of the Andy Petree Racing team, the future once again looks bright. Wallace put together his best year as a professional in 1999, claiming three top-five finishes in the No. 55 Square D Chevrolet.

FULL THROTTLE

Jeff Gordon's rookie season in Winston Cup competition raced past in a dream-like blur. And before his veteran competitors could wipe the sleep from their eyes, the kid established himself as the new face of NASCAR.

Gordon, crew chief Ray Evernham, team owner Rick Hendrick and the rest of the Rainbow Warriors began the 1994 season well, starting sixth and finishing fourth behind Sterling Marlin in the Daytona 500.

Gordon continued to post some good showings, but it wasn't until the Coca-Cola 600 at

By Johnny D. Boggs

Charlotte Motor Speedway on Memorial Day weekend that he proved his rookie season had been no fluke.

He had recorded success at the 1.5-mile superspeedway before, winning the pole in the fall Winston Cup race in 1993 and claiming both poles and checkered flags in his 1992 Busch season. In 1994 Gordon put the No. 24 DuPont Automotive Finishes Chevrolet on the pole for

A victory in the 1994 Coca-Cola at Charlotte prompted tears of joy from Jeff and his mother, Carol Bickford.

the six-hundred-mile race as well, then held off Rusty Wallace and Geoff Bodine to score the first Winston Cup victory of his career. Tears flowed freely as Gordon took the trophy in victory lane.

Six weeks later, he would be overcome by emotion again. Indianapolis Motor Speedway had been playing host to the Indianapolis 500 since 1911. But this year, for the first time, NASCAR was coming to the "Brickyard." For Gordon, who had gone to high school in nearby

Gordon enjoyed success both on and off the track in 1994. Jeff finished eighth in the Winston Cup points standings, and when he and Brooke tied the knot in November, it was the NASCAR version of a Royal Wedding.

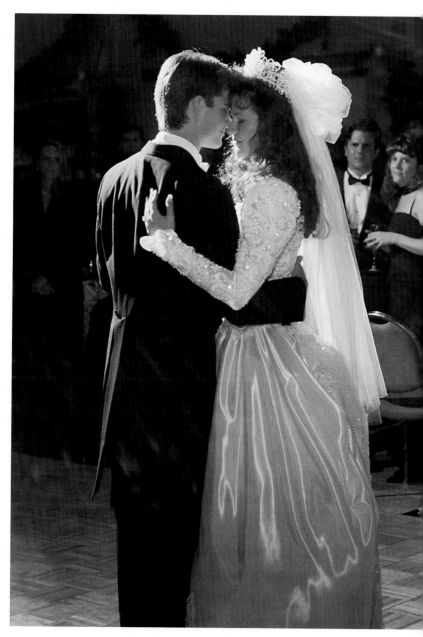

Pittsboro, this would be a home-coming before thousands of screaming fans.

Gordon started third behind surprising pole winner Rick Mast on August 6. As the race wound down, it became a two-man duel between Ernie Irvan and the home-town favorite. But with about four laps to go, Irvan's Ford developed tire problems and Gordon shot around and took the checkered flag. Crying again, Gordon — just two days past his twenty-third birthday — needed two victory laps to pull himself together.

"That was one race where you looked at it like, 'Wow! NASCAR wrote the script on this one to the last letter,'" says John Sturbin, motorsports reporter for the *Fort Worth Star-Telegram*. "It was just so perfect. . . . He was crying again, and I was like, 'What is it with this guy? Maybe he is a kid.' But he didn't know how good he was going to be."

The fairy tale was just beginning. Jeff finished eighth in the Winston Cup points standings that year and claimed $1,779,523 in race winnings. Evernham was voted crew chief of the year. And on November 26, Jeff married Brooke Sealey at First Baptist Church in Charlotte.

Jeff held off Dale Earnhardt for the victory at Rockingham, then, for good measure, edged the Intimidator for the 1995 Cup championship.

Gordon quickly established himself as a favorite for the Winston Cup title in 1995 by winning the season's second race at Rockingham. Six victories and four runner-up finishes later, Jeff became the youngest Cup champion since Bill Rexford in 1950.

Gordon had recorded a year that would be hard to surpass, but he'd find a way to do just that in 1995.

After scoring his first victory of the 1995 season at Rockingham in the second Cup race of the year, Gordon followed that with victories at Atlanta, Bristol, Daytona and New Hampshire.

With nine races left in the season, the twenty-four-year-old found himself with a 176-point lead over Sterling Marlin in the Winston Cup points race and a big test looming: the Southern 500 at Darlington Raceway, the track "too tough to tame." Marlin had won the spring race at the fabled track that year.

"He took to this place with the Winston Cup about like you do a new pair of jeans," Darlington Raceway president Jim Hunter says of Gordon. "You know . . . a perfect fit."

Gordon battled Dale Jarrett, Dale Earnhardt and Rusty Wallace to come away with the victory and

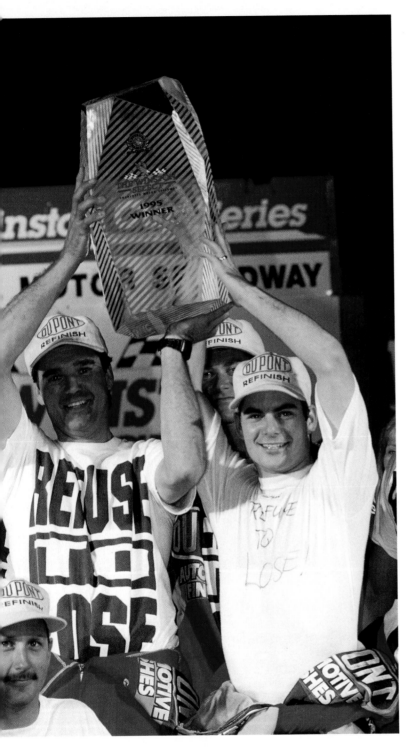

In addition to seven points victories in '95, Jeff was victorious in the Winston Select all-star race at Charlotte, winning all three segments.

a 217-point lead over Marlin. After a sixth-place posting at Richmond, Gordon dominated the MBNA 500 at Dover Downs in Delaware, leading four hundred of the five hundred laps for his seventh win.

In the end, Gordon won the Cup championship over Earnhardt by thirty-four points (Marlin placed third). In addition to his seven victories, Gordon posted four runner-up finishes, eight poles and took home $4,347,343 in winnings, becoming the youngest Cup champion in the post-1972 "Modern Era" and the youngest ever since twenty-three-year-old Bill Rexford in 1950.

Gordon added ten Cup victories, five poles and $3,428,485 in prize money in 1996, but Hendrick Motorsports teammate Terry Labonte captured the Cup championship that year despite posting only two wins. Gordon wouldn't complain about NASCAR's points scoring system, however, which

Gordon, Terry Labonte (center) and Ken Schrader (right) formed NASCAR's version of the Dream Team until 1997 when Schrader joined Andy Petree Racing.

awards consistency as much as, if not more than, victories. He still had plenty of success, sweeping the Darlington and Dover races and finishing second in the points competition. And 1997 would be, in Gordon's word, "awesome."

During NASCAR's 50th anniversary season, Gordon and the Rainbow Warriors continued their "Refuse to Lose" slogan. Gordon

made history at Darlington when he won the Southern 500 to become only the second driver to claim the Winston Million bonus. The prize was awarded to any driver who could win three of NASCAR's four "crown jewel" races (Daytona 500,

Above: Gordon was unstoppable in 1997 en route to his second points championship. A year after posting seven victories but still losing out on the Cup championship to Hendrick teammate Terry Labonte, Jeff scored ten victories and earned a record $6,375,658 in earnings.

Left: Jeff became only the second driver to win the Winston Million bonus in 1997 when he claimed a hard-fought victory over Jeff Burton in the Southern 500. The prize was awarded to any driver who could win three of NASCAR's four "crown jewel" races.

Coca-Cola 600, Winston 500, Southern 500) in a season. Jeff's victory was hard-fought as he and Jeff Burton traded paint while battling side by side on the final lap of the race.

When the season ended, Gordon had scored ten victories, a record $6,375,658 in winnings, and, most importantly, his second Cup

Gordon raised the bar again in 1998, tying Richard Petty's modern-era mark with thirteen wins and raking in more than $9 million in purse money. He tied another NASCAR mark with four consecutive wins en route to becoming the youngest three-time Cup champ.

championship. How could he top that?

Well, try this: In '98 he posted thirteen victories, tying Richard Petty's modern-era mark set in 1975; six second-place finishes; seven poles; and $9,306,584 in purse money. He won four consecutive times, tying another NASCAR record, and became the youngest three-time Cup champion.

After Gordon won an unprecedented fourth consecutive Southern 500 that year, a reporter asked if there were any more big victories for him to win. In true Gordon fashion, he said he considered them all big victories. And when someone asked for his autograph after the

interview session, Gordon quipped: "You know it's a big victory when someone in the press box asks for your autograph."

By the time the 1999 season rolled around, Gordon had amassed more than $26 million in Winston Cup prize money. He even started a Busch team with Ray Evernham, running a limited schedule in the No. 24 Pepsi Monte Carlo.

Gordon opened the Cup season with a Daytona 500 victory, but 1999 would not be his year to tie Cale Yarborough's record of three consecutive Winston Cup championships. He took one of his hardest hits when he wrecked at Texas Motor Speedway, and although he kept winning races, he was all but

Gordon's bid for a third consecutive points title in 1999 began with a victory in the Daytona 500, but inconsistency and a wreck at Texas Motor Speedway kept him from making a serious run at eventual champion Dale Jarrett.

Right: Jeff and new crew chief Brian Whitesell teamed for back-to-back victories in the NAPA Autocare 500 and UAW/GM Quality 500, immediately quashing any doubts that Gordon couldn't win without his mentor, Ray Evernham.

Below: Rick Hendrick reaffirmed his commitment to Gordon on the heels of Evernham's departure, announcing a long-term agreement in which Gordon became an equity partner in the Hendrick No. 24 team.

Much of Gordon's success in 2000 may hinge on how the Rainbow Warriors deal with the defection of five members to the Robert Yates team.

mathematically out of the points race by the time Dale Jarrett won the Pepsi 400 at Daytona in July.

Perhaps Gordon's biggest challenge came September 28 when Evernham, his longtime crew chief, resigned to form his own team. How could Gordon fare without his mentor and friend? Was the magic gone?

Not hardly. New crew chief Brian Whitesell's decision not to bring Gordon in on a late caution-flag pit stop gave Gordon the lead in their first race, and Gordon held off Dale Earnhardt to win at Martinsville, Virginia. The Gordon-Whitesell duo followed that with a victory in Charlotte.

Gordon has proven he has plenty to give NASCAR — and isn't about to rest on his laurels. As

Darlington president Jim Hunter says: "I think as long as he has the desire that he currently has . . . he is going to be the man in NASCAR racing."

TRADING PAINT

Jeff Gordon is tough. He's a great competitor. He may not look tough, and he may sound like a polite kid, but believe me, on a racetrack, he's as tough as they come.

He has that competitive nature, and I think, like most champion racers, you can see it in everything he does. I don't care whether it's racing, computer games, or whatever he does, he's competitive. And that's why he's a winner. He goes that extra mile, and he works hard.

Gordon is not a young driver, at least not in terms of experience. When you add up all the

By Dale Earnhardt
As Told To Monte Dutton

Above: Earnhardt says not to let Jeff's smaller stature and good looks fool you: ". . . on a racetrack, he's as tough as they come."

Below: Jeff's years of racing experience was evident in the 1998 Pepsi 400. Gordon went with a two-tire change in his last pit stop and then proceeded to catch Mark Martin for his record fourth consecutive Cup victory.

years Jeff has been in racing, beginning in go-karts, he's been around a long time. He had a lot of experience when he got here to NASCAR.

He grew into it. Down South here, most guys don't start racing until they're sixteen or seventeen years old. In the Midwest, and the West where he came from, they start racing quarter midgets and go-karts when they are five or six years old. He had quite a bit of time in a seat, and I don't care whether it's racing go-karts or Cup cars, you get that instinct about racing that you need to win.

Racing is racing, and I don't buy into the notion that a guy who

comes up in one kind of racing can't excel in another. That doesn't mean that I'm going to go Indy-car racing tomorrow, or that I ever wanted to, but it means that a real good driver who has made a name for himself is capable of getting the hang of another kind of racing.

Earnhardt sought the advice of racing legends David Pearson, Bobby Allison and Richard Petty as an up-and-coming driver. Now he's glad to share his knowledge with Gordon.

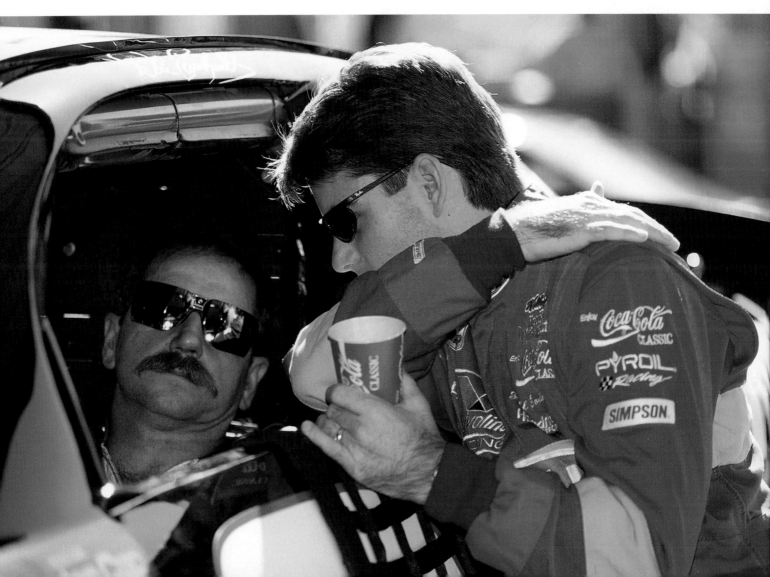

Once Gordon takes over the lead in a race, he rarely relinquishes it.

No competitor, not even a determined Jeff Burton, could keep an exhausted Gordon from claiming the Winston No Bull 5 $1 million bonus at Darlington in 1998.

Dale Jr. came up through the ranks driving stock cars, and I believe that's been an excellent preparation for him. I don't think what he's done with his career has done anything but help him, and now he's about to become a regular competitor in Winston Cup (beginning in the 2000 season).

The way Gordon came up was an excellent preparation for him. He was racing, and it was challenging enough that it helped him get better. The important factor there is competition. The only kind of racing that's not good for you is racing that's too easy — or finding yourself with equipment that's not up to snuff. If the racing is competitive, and the equipment is good enough to let you develop your skills, then you've got the opportunity to become a racer.

Now Jeff's won three Winston Cup championships, and yes, it's incredible for a guy to have achieved all that by the time he's twenty-eight years old.

I got to know him when he was in Busch. Don Hawk (Earnhardt's business manager) and (Gordon's stepfather John) Bickford and I got to know each other. We talked a lot about racing and the business side of it.

Gordon's a guy who is always thinking. When he asks you a question, he really listens to what you have to say. People who think someone else is calling the shots have got

it all wrong. He's very knowledge-able on the whole sport of racing, whether it's the racing or the business side of it.

We all have people we look up to, people we respect and learn from when it's early in our careers. For me, it was great to learn from

"When you're in this business, what really makes it fun is racing with the guys you respect. Gordon's good, and I respect his ability." — Dale Earnhardt

guys such as David Pearson, Bobby Allison and Richard Petty. When Gordon came along, if he wanted to talk to me and pick my brain on something, whether it was on the track or off it, I was glad to help him.

It was good that he wanted to talk to me and other guys who had been here before he came. Gordon respects what I've done, and I appreciate that about him.

Jeff focuses on one thing once he straps himself into a race car: winning.

Most of the people who don't like Gordon are people who don't know him. He's a good guy, and he's someone who hasn't let all that success and money go to his head. If the fans give him a hard time, well, that's just something you've got to expect.

If you're a Dale Earnhardt fan, a Dale Jarrett fan, a Mark Martin fan, or whoever, you're not going to be happy when Jeff Gordon wins the race. I really believe he understands that, so a lot more is made

A Tradition In The Earnhardt Garage For Over 40 Years

Much of the anti-Gordon sentiment comes from loyal Earnhardt fans, but Dale says he believes Jeff understands: "If you're a Dale Earnhardt fan, a Dale Jarrett fan, a Mark Martin fan, or whoever, you're not going to be happy when Jeff Gordon wins the race."

out of it by others than I think is really made out of it by him.

Gordon's got his fans, and there are a lot of them. I went through the same thing. Darrell (Waltrip) went through the same thing. It's not like a football game, where one group is pulling for one team and the another group is pulling for the other. There are forty-three cars on the racetrack, and with all his success, he's kind of become the threat to the fans of all forty-two of the others.

To fans who blame risky driving by Gordon for Earnhardt's crash at the 1997 Daytona 500, the Intimidator says "that's a bunch of bull."

In that kind of a situation, you're going to get booed, and the fans have that right. They paid their way in, and being willing to do that is what keeps the rest of us in business.

I think he's really learned and become somebody who can win a race, and all of a sudden, take care and win on the business side of it too. He is his own man there, too. Anybody who thinks he just sits back there in the background and counts his money has got it all wrong.

I've had some business dealings with him, and just being friends and being with him in racing, he has that competitive spirit. He doesn't come off that way just looking at him and talking to him on things, but he's serious about what he does, whether he's involved in business with you or racing against you.

Sometimes people mention the 1997 Daytona 500, when Gordon and I were racing, and he went up by me when we were coming off the second turn. I got a little loose, Jarrett got into me and I wrecked. Gordon went on and won the race.

People have suggested that it was kind of a rash move on his part, and that it surprised me because I didn't think he would make that move at that particular point in the race. They make out like the wreck was his fault or something like that.

Well, that's a bunch of bull. He made a move because we were racing. It wasn't the reason I wrecked; it was just racing. It was one of those things that happens sometimes. He won the Daytona 500 that year, and I won it the next year.

When you're in this business, what really makes it fun is racing with the guys you respect. Gordon's good, and I respect his ability. He respects mine. It doesn't get any

better than when you know you're racing against someone who is one of the best.

That's rivalry.

Dale Earnhardt *and Jeff Gordon may have been involved in a controversial crash at the 1997 Daytona, but when their cars collided after the 1999 event, it was all in good fun.*

Knowing the winner's car is kept by NASCAR for its Daytona USA attraction, Earnhardt pulled next to Gordon following his victory, scuffed the shiny No. 24 car with his tire and waved before driving off.

It probably won't be the last time the two competitors bump into each other on a racetrack. Earnhardt, a record seven-time winner of the Winston Cup series, isn't ready to retire just yet. And three-time winner Gordon is just hitting his prime.

"I like to race him and beat him, I tell you that," Earnhardt says.

COMMERCIAL BREAK

It's not unusual these days to see three-time Winston Cup champion Darrell Waltrip touting Route 66 blue jeans during a commercial break on a broadcast network in primetime. He's even turned up in a commercial spot for Wendy's wearing his Kmart team uniform.

A decade ago, it would have been unheard of to see Waltrip, Dale Earnhardt, or even seven-time champion Richard Petty, on a national prime-time commercial.

Then again, Jeff Gordon wasn't associated with NASCAR a decade ago.

In a relatively short period of time on the

By Richard Huff

Jeff's motor home provides seclusion from the daily rigors — and adoring fans — during each race week.

Winston Cup circuit, Gordon has proven to be an outstanding driver on the track and an exceptionally well handled marketing property away from the asphalt. Armed with a top-flight management team, Gordon has revolutionized the marketing of NASCAR drivers.

"He was one of the first to really be utilized in national campaigns," says racing historian Bob Latford, author of *Built for Speed:*

The Ultimate Guide to Stock Car Racetracks. "It was partially because of his looks and partially because of his success. He's articulate, he's good looking and the kid drives well."

Before Gordon came along, Winston Cup drivers were considered subspecies in the sporting world. Sponsors would use drivers in television commercials, but not in spots that ran outside stock car racing telecasts. The national spots, those that turned up in the Super

Bowl or even during *Friends*, always starred mainstream, stick-and-ball athletes.

But a few years back, Pepsi, which had then recently lured Gordon from rival Coca-Cola, incorporated the driver into a national campaign that placed him alongside the likes of Shaquille O'Neal and Deion Sanders. In a heartbeat, or more like the length of a thirty-second spot, Gordon transcended motorsports and became a full-fledged sports superstar.

Fans of the sport have always considered the drivers national athletes. It was just that marketing mavens, the bigwigs that control the advertising bucks on Madison Avenue, hadn't considered drivers worthy of coast-to-coast attention.

At home, Gordon prefers not to watch, talk about, or even think about, racing — unless he's playing video games with Brooke.

Jeff also recharges his batteries by playing basketball, working out, enjoying water sports — or when there's not enough time to hit the lake — playing with his custom No. 24 remote control boat.

"All of American sports look for heroes to drive the public's attention and to get the interest of causal viewers and spectators," explains Neal Pilson, head of Pilson Communications, a consulting agency that does work for NASCAR. "Mark McGwire and Sammy Sosa drove up the ratings and marketing for baseball. Michael Jordan is the best example of a personality lifting a sport. Jeff Gordon is doing a lot of the same for NASCAR."

Gordon and his team have parlayed his appeal into a multi-million dollar operation, spanning direct sponsor tie-ins, a Website (www.jeffgordon.com), licensing and the like. In short, Gordon is NASCAR's Tiger Woods: young, handsome, and a legend well ahead of his years.

Fact is, in a short period of time, he's gone from being an outstanding upstart driver to a stand-alone corporation. Gordon may

Not all of Gordon's sponsorships prove to be self-serving. Here Jeff pours himself a bowl of cereal at Morningside Elementary School in Atlanta on March 9, 1999, helping to promote National School Breakfast Week in addition to the launch of Kellogg's K'-Sentials.

actually have come along at just the right time. A few years earlier, and, well, maybe the level of off-track success wouldn't be the same.

Certainly, at the time Waltrip won his championships, he was every bit as marketable as Gordon

At 24, I became the second youngest champion in NASCAR history. Here's another little-known fact. Of the 42 drivers who chase me at more than 200 mph, most don't get enough calcium. My advice? Drink three glasses of milk a day. Preferably while standing still.

MILK
Where's your mustache?"

Above: Got milk? Only if you're one of the more recognizable faces in sports. Other famous milk mustaches include Mark McGwire, Brett Favre and Cal Ripken Jr.

Right: In a December 14, 1998, article titled "Heir Gordon," Forbes magazine labeled Jeff one of the most sought-after endorsers in professional sports "behind only Michael Jordan, Tiger Woods and Arnold Palmer."

a respectable sports event. Coverage was limited to snippets on ABC's *Wide World of Sports*. Heck, the first national start-to-finish television coverage of a race didn't occur until 1979.

But television changed everything. Now every race is carried live nationally, bringing the stars of NASCAR into the homes of millions.

Gordon has also benefited from the decades-long stereotype of stock car drivers as tobacco-spitting Southerners with unintelligible drawls. While race fans know well the stereotype is false, advertising executives have been slow to come to terms with this fact. Compared to the stereotype, Gordon stuck out. He didn't speak with a twang and carried himself in a distinguished manner on and off the track.

"Jeff Gordon has an appeal that goes beyond the core NASCAR

is today. He was young, well groomed and extremely articulate. Yet in the early seventies, racing had yet to gain national attention as

"Jeff Gordon has an appeal that goes beyond the core NASCAR audience. He's brash. He is not from the same background as many of the other drivers. He is helping NASCAR reach new levels of popularity." — Neal Pilson, Pilson Communications

audience," Pilson says. "He's brash. He is not from the same background as many of the other drivers. He is helping NASCAR reach new levels of popularity." Indeed, Gordon was the first and so far only Winston Cup driver to be named one of *People* magazine's fifty most-beautiful people.

Early on, advertisers bought into the Gordon mystique in a major way, buying into his DuPont-backed Hendrick Motorsports team and into the driver's company itself. A few years ago, he was answering to about thirty different corporations, each funneling money into the operation. In return, these corporations each got to use Gordon's image on their products in an attempt to lure loyal fans.

Being popular does have some downside, though. When you're on top, everyone wants a piece of the action, which usually requires time. And while racing only takes place on weekends, most drivers spend a sizeable portion of their weekdays dealing with sponsor and off-the-track issues.

Following Gordon's 1997 title win, he and his management team decided to avoid burnout and cut back a bit on his sponsor involvement. By the end of 1998, they'd whittled their sponsor companies down to about twenty blue-chip clients such as Pepsi and Edy's Ice Cream.

Likewise, rather than do numerous signings at car dealerships around the country, Gordon & Co. have targeted appearances where fans may get a bit closer and better experience. There may be nothing worse for a driver's reputation than to have way too many people sign up for an autograph signing. Someone will ultimately go home unhappy and complain about the experience, which reflects badly on the driver.

Instead, Gordon now does events where he can field questions from fans. His Website, which provides weekly updates on races as well as some tie-ins with his sponsors, is another tool he uses to reach fans.

Major events in his schedule are planned out nearly a year in advance, which gives Gordon a chance to pencil in some free time and provides his management team with a clear picture for the future.

Considering his schedule, there isn't much time for quality time at home during the racing season. Because of his popularity, it's a bit difficult for Jeff and wife Brooke to go out without being noticed. To that end, constant fan attention at his home in North Carolina forced the Gordons to seek a less busy neighborhood in Florida.

NASCAR fans are more loyal than fans of any other sport. According to a 1997 study by Performance Research, seventy-two percent of racing fans say they first look for goods made by NASCAR sponsors.

The media horde has grown steadily
during Gordon's incredible string of
successes throughout the past decade.

One day a week is usually set aside to do nothing.

"It's a hectic life," he once told *Inside NASCAR* magazine. "A lot of times we both wish we had more time with just the two of us. But at the same time, it's a great lifestyle. It has its benefits."

When he's not racing, Gordon can be found playing video games — he's an avid player — boating, going to restaurants or simply relaxing with Brooke.

Outside of social activities, Gordon also devotes some of his time to charitable ventures, such as raising awareness for bone marrow donors.

Nevertheless, there are times when he's got to get away. The Gordons schedule regular vacations on off-weeks during the season and immediately following the last race of the year.

"I think with as much racing that I do, and that I've done over the years, it's a very essential part of my life to take a vacation where I don't read or hear anything about racing," he told *Inside NASCAR*.

And if he's away and something about racing appears on television, he'll leave the room. "I've got to totally get away," he said.

Despite the occasional hassles involved and the constant stress, Gordon doesn't plan to leave the sport anytime soon. Likewise, drivers will no doubt follow the path he's blazed during the nineties for years to come.

"Though he didn't come around until the middle of the nineties, he's an important figure," says Latford. "He has kind of set the pattern we're seeing others follow. He puts a positive image of an athlete in front of a lot of people who don't follow racing."

WINNER'S CIRCLE

J eff Gordon is one of the best drivers of all time. His success — forty-nine Winston Cup victories through the 1999 season — has shown that. The thing about Jeff Gordon is that he's so good on and off the track.

He's a perfect role model for young people. Everybody in the world wants him to do advertising for them. They want him to come speak. They want all of these things.

Our former crew chief, Ray Evernham, put a great team together at Hendrick Motorsports, and it takes a great team to achieve success. But Jeff

By John Hendrick
As Told To Tom Gillispie

has unbelievable talent. We've seen it with all of his wins over the last six years. This team's only going to get better, and Jeff's got an unbelievable talent that will keep him in the top of the sport.

There are younger and younger drivers coming up, and many of them are coming up because of Jeff. Look at the year that Tony Stewart's had in 1999, probably the best rookie year ever in Winston Cup. (Stewart notched three victories and finished fourth in the overall standings.) We get information from drivers thirteen, fourteen, fifteen, sixteen years old now, and they all want to get close to Jeff. They all want to know Jeff. So his success has helped bring younger people into this sport.

"He gives all the credit to God, and that's the perfect role model for a mom or dad worried about their son or daughter." — John Hendrick

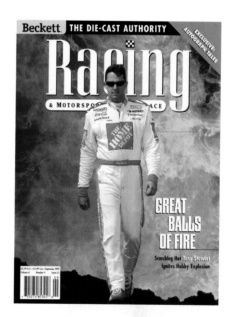

Jeff's success has paved the way for other young, talented drivers such as Tony Stewart. Stewart set the NASCAR circuit ablaze during a record-setting rookie season, posting three victories and twelve top-five finishes.

Jeff goes to churches to give his testimony, and who knows how many people show up when he goes to do something like that? He gives all the credit to God, and that's the perfect role model for a mom or dad worried about their son or daughter.

I don't know that there's pressure on Jeff to carry the sport, but I guess Jeff does put pressure on himself to win. Certainly, he wants to win today, and he wants to win next week.

It's not easy being Jeff

The love-hate relationship is so strong with Gordon that there are dozens of anti-Gordon sites on the Internet. Hendrick says Gordon's victories have become so routine that many fans are just looking for change: "He's won three of the last four Winston Cup championships and finished second the other year. It's because he's so successful that [fans are] tired of seeing him win."

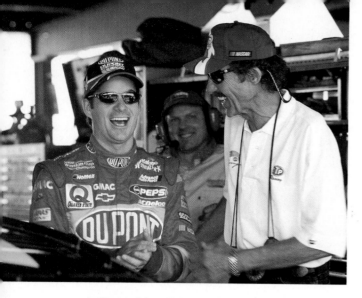

Jeff would still have to average ten victories a season over the next fifteen Winston Cup seasons to catch Richard Petty. The King has won a record two hundred races.

Gordon. I think the booing bothers Jeff, but like Dale Earnhardt says, as long as they're doing something — booing or cheering — don't worry about it. Mark Martin and Dale Earnhardt both have said in newspaper or magazine articles that it hurt them when they got booed. You're either Jeff Gordon fans or you're not.

A lot of fans are tired of him winning. They don't want him to win. He's won three of the last four Winston Cup championships and finished second the other year. It's because he's so successful that they're tired of seeing him win.

Dale Earnhardt is the only driver besides Petty to claim seven Winston Cup championships.

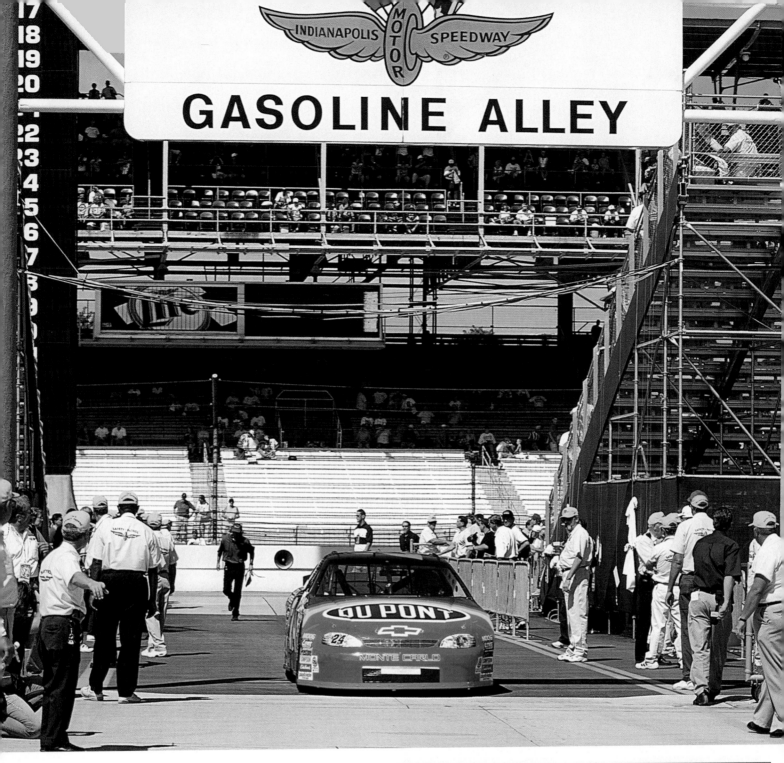

Whatever legacy Gordon leaves behind, his name always will be synonymous with the Brickyard 400. Gordon won the inaugural event in 1994 and again in 1998.

Gordon claimed seven Bud Poles in 1999, bringing his career Winston Cup poles total to thirty.

Jeff's future now is in the hands of veteran crew chief Robbie Loomis, who made the move from Richard Petty Enterprises once interim crew chief Brian Whitesell was promoted to the position of team manager.

They don't want to see him win another championship, and, certainly, all of those Earnhardt fans don't want to see him catch Earnhardt and his seven championships.

Is he the top race car driver of all time? Only time will tell that, with Dale Earnhardt, Richard Petty and all of those guys, but Jeff has such a strong talent.

I'm a big supporter of Jeff

John Hendrick respects Jeff even more as a driver, and person, since taking over as president and CEO of Hendrick Motorsports.

Gordon, for what he's meant to me the last two years when my brother, Rick, was sick. Ray Evernham, Jeff Gordon, Terry Labonte and others have been a big help to me. Jeff made me comfortable. He made it clear: "John, I want you to be there when Rick's not there." He and I have a great relationship.

Jeff's a great race car driver, but I've gotten to know him, and he's just a great guy, too.

John Hendrick, *president and CEO of Hendrick Motorsports, didn't take to racing quite as quickly as his brother, Rick. For John, becoming director of the most successful NASCAR team in the business was a lifelong journey.*

While Rick was building a solid foundation in racing, John attended college, earning a bachelor's degree in science at the University of Cincinnati, and worked in a family business. But with Rick's prodding, John attended a training program in automotive management and eventually became a dealer.

When Rick struggled through legal problems and began treatments for leukemia in 1997, John took over the day-to-day duties of Hendrick Motorsports.

The company never missed a beat. Hendrick cars swept the top three spots in the early-season Daytona 500, and Gordon charged to the Winston Cup championship — the Hendrick team's third consecutive season title.

Jeff has raced with more than twenty different paint schemes in the 1990s, plugging everything from Star Wars to Superman.

CAREER RECORD

Year	Starts	Wins	2nd	3rd	4th	5th	6-10th	11-35th	DNFs	Poles	Outside Poles	Total Earned
1992	1	0	0	0	0	0	0	0	1	0	0	$6,285
1993	30	0	2	1	1	3	4	8	11	1	0	$765,168
1994	31	2	1	1	2	1	7	7	10	1	1	$1,779,523
1995	31	7	4	5	0	1	6	5	3	8	3	$4,347,343
1996	31	10	3	4	2	2	3	2	5	5	10	$3,428,485
1997	32	10	3	2	4	3	1	7	2	1	3	$6,375,658
1998	33	13	6	3	1	3	2	3	2	7	4	$9,306,584
1999	34	7	4	6	1	1	3	7	7	7	3	$5,281,361
Totals	**223**	**49**	**23**	**22**	**11**	**14**	**26**	**39**	**41**	**30**	**24**	**$31,290,707**

CAREER VICTORIES

Date	Event	Track	Type	Make	Finish	Start	Laps	Status	Earnings
5/29/94	Coca-Cola 600	Charlotte	SS	Chevrolet	1	1	400	Running	$196,500
8/6/94	Brickyard 400	Indianapolis	SS	Chevrolet	1	3	160	Running	$613,000
2/26/95	Goodwrench 500	Rockingham	SS	Chevrolet	1	1	492	Running	$167,600
3/12/95	Purolator 500	Atlanta	SS	Chevrolet	1	3	328	Running	$104,950
4/2/95	Food City 500	Bristol	ST	Chevrolet	1	2	500	Running	$67,645
7/1/95	Pepsi 400	Daytona	SS	Chevrolet	1	3	160	Running	$96,580
7/9/95	Slick 50 300	New Hampshire	SS	Chevrolet	1	21	300	Running	$160,300
9/3/95	Mountain Dew Southern 500	Darlington	SS	Chevrolet	1	5	367	Running	$70,630
9/17/95	MBNA 500	Dover	SS	Chevrolet	1	2	500	Running	$74,655
3/3/96	Pontiac Excitement 400	Richmond	ST	Chevrolet	1	2	400	Running	$92,400
3/24/96	TranSouth Financial 400	Darlington	SS	Chevrolet	1	2	293	Running	$97,310
3/31/96	Food City 500	Bristol	ST	Chevrolet	1	8	500	Running	$93,765
6/2/96	Miller 500	Dover	SS	Chevrolet	1	1	500	Running	$138,730
6/16/96	UAW-GM Teamwork 500	Pocono	SS	Chevrolet	1	1	200	Running	$96,980
7/28/96	DieHard 500	Talladega	SS	Chevrolet	1	2	188	Running	$272,550
9/1/96	Mountain Dew Southern 500	Darlington	SS	Chevrolet	1	2	367	Running	$99,630
9/15/96	MBNA 500	Dover	SS	Chevrolet	1	3	500	Running	$153,630
9/22/96	Hanes 500	Martinsville	ST	Chevrolet	1	10	500	Running	$93,825
9/29/96	Tyson Holly Farms 400	N. Wilkesbro	St	Chevrolet	1	2	400	Running	$91,350
2/16/97	Daytona 500	Daytona	SS	Chevrolet	1	6	200	Running	$456,999
2/23/97	GM Goodwrench Service Plus 400	Rockingham	SS	Chevrolet	1	4	393	Running	$93,115
4/13/97	Food City 500	Bristol	ST	Chevrolet	1	5	500	Running	$83,640
4/20/97	Goody's 500	Martinsville	ST	Chevrolet	1	4	500	Running	$99,225
5/17/97	The Winston Select	Charlotte	SS	Chevrolet	1	19	70	Running	$207,500
5/25/97	Coca-Cola 600	Charlotte	SS	Chevrolet	1	1	400	Running	$224,900
6/8/97	Pocono 500	Pocono	SS	Chevrolet	1	11	200	Running	$166,080
6/22/97	NAPA's California 500	Fontana	SS	Chevrolet	1	3	250	Running	$144,600
8/10/97	The Bud at the Glenn	Watkins Glenn	RC	Chevrolet	1	11	90	Running	$139,120
8/31/97	Mountain Dew Southern 500	Darlington	SS	Chevrolet	1	7	367	Running	$1,131,330
9/14/97	New Hampshire 300	New Hampshire	SS	Chevrolet	1	13	300	Running	$188,625
2/22/98	GM Goodwrench Service Plus 400	Rockingham	SS	Chevrolet	1	4	393	Running	$90,090
3/29/98	Food City 500	Bristol	ST	Chevrolet	1	2	500	Running	$90,860
5/24/98	Coca-Cola 600	Charlotte	SS	Chevrolet	1	1	400	Running	$346,450
6/28/98	Save Mart/Kragen 350	Sears Point	RC	Chevrolet	1	1	112	Running	$160,675

Date	Event	Track	Type	Make	Finish	Start	Laps	Status	Earnings
7/26/98	Pennsylvania 500	Pocono	SS	Chevrolet	1	2	200	Running	$162,770
8/1/98	Brickyard 400	Indianapolis	SS	Chevrolet	1	3	160	Running	$637,625
8/9/98	The Bud at the Glenn	Watkins Glen	RC	Chevrolet	1	1	90	Running	$152,970
8/16/98	Pepsi 400 by DeVilbliss	Michigan	SS	Chevrolet	1	3	200	Running	$120,302
8/30/98	Farm Aid on CMT 300	New Hampshire	SS	Chevrolet	1	1	300	Running	$205,400
9/6/98	Pepsi Southern 400	Darlington	SS	Chevrolet	1	5	367	Running	$134,655
10/17/98	Pepsi 400	Daytona	SS	Chevrolet	1	8	160	Running	$184,325
11/1/98	AC Delco 400	Rockingham	SS	Chevrolet	1	9	393	Running	$111,575
11/8/98	NAPA 500	Atlanta	SS	Chevrolet	1	21	221	Running	$164,450
2/14/99	Daytona 500	Daytona	SS	Chevrolet	1	1	200	Running	$2,194,246
3/14/99	Cracker Barrel 500	Atlanta	SS	Chevrolet	1	8	325	Running	$117,650
5/2/99	California 500 Presented by NAPA	California	SS	Chevrolet	1	5	250	Running	$155,890
6/27/99	Save Mart/Kragen 350	Sears Point	RC	Chevrolet	1	1	112	Running	$125,040
8/15/99	Frontier at the Glenn	Watkins Glenn	RC	Chevrolet	1	3	90	Running	$119,860
10/3/99	NAPA Autocare 500	Martinsville	St	Chevrolet	1	5	500	Running	$110,090

CAREER POLES

Date	Event	Track	Type	Make	Finish	Start	Laps	Status
10/10/93	Mello Yello 500	Charlotte	SS	Chevrolet	5	1	334	Running
5/29/94	Coca-Cola 600	Charlotte	SS	Chevrolet	1	1	400	Running
2/26/95	Goodwrench 500	Rockingham	SS	Chevrolet	1	1	492	Running
3/5/95	Pontiac Excitement 400	Richmond	ST	Chevrolet	36	1	183	Fuel Pump
3/26/95	TranSouth Financial 400	Darlington	SS	Chevrolet	32	1	200	Accident
4/9/95	First Union 400	N. Wilkesbro	ST	Chevrolet	2	1	400	Running
5/28/95	Coca-Cola 600	Charlotte	SS	Chevrolet	33	1	283	Suspension
6/4/95	Miller Genuine Draft 500	Dover	SS	Chevrolet	6	1	499	Running
6/18/95	Miller Genuine Draft 400	Michigan	SS	Chevrolet	2	1	200	Running
8/5/95	Brickyard 400	Indianapolis	SS	Chevrolet	6	1	160	Running
5/26/96	Coca-Cola 600	Charlotte	SS	Chevrolet	4	1	400	Running
6/2/96	Miller 500	Dover	SS	Chevrolet	1	1	500	Running
6/16/96	UAW-GM Teamwork 500	Pocono	SS	Chevrolet	1	1	200	Running
7/6/96	Pepsi 400	Daytona	SS	Chevrolet	3	1	160	Running
8/3/96	Brickyard 400	Indianapolis	SS	Chevrolet	37	1	40	Accident
5/25/97	Coca-Cola 600	Charlotte	SS	Chevrolet	1	1	400	Running
5/3/98	California 500	Fontana	SS	Chevrolet	4	1	250	Running
5/24/98	Coca-Cola 600	Charlotte	SS	Chevrolet	1	1	400	Running
6/6/98	Pontiac Excitement 400	Richmond	ST	Chevrolet	37	1	372	Accident
6/21/98	Pocono 500	Pocono	SS	Chevrolet	2	1	200	Running
6/28/98	Save Mart/Kragen 350	Sears Point	RC	Chevrolet	1	1	112	Running
8/9/98	The Bud at the Glenn	Watkins Glen	RC	Chevrolet	1	1	90	Running
8/30/98	Farm Aid on CMT 300	New Hampshire	SS	Chevrolet	1	1	300	Running
2/14/99	Daytona 500	Daytona	SS	Chevrolet	1	1	200	Running
3/21/99	TranSouth Financial 400	Darlington	SS	Chevrolet	3	1	164	Running
5/15/99	Pontiac Excitement 400	Richmond	ST	Chevrolet	31	1	388	Running
6/13/99	K-Mart 400	Michigan	SS	Chevrolet	2	1	200	Running
6/27/99	Save Mart/Kragen 350	Sears Point	RC	Chevrolet	1	1	112	Running
7/11/99	Jiffy Lube 300	New Hampshire	SS	Chevrolet	3	1	300	Running
8/7/99	Brickyard 400	Indianapolis	SS	Chevrolet	3	1	160	Running

Source: *NASCAR Winston Cup Series Media Guide*

LOOK FOR THESE OTHER QUALITY RACING BOOKS FROM BECKETT PUBLICATIONS.

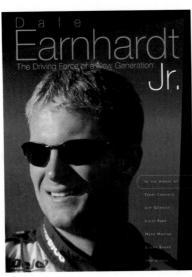

Dale Earnhardt Jr.:
The Driving Force of a New Generation

The Intimidator's son is on his way to making a name for himself in NASCAR. This beautifully photographed book includes chapters told in the words of the people who know Dale Jr. best. Veteran racer Mark Martin comments on Jr.'s study of the sport. And the legendary Buddy Baker compares famous father and fast-rising son. And there are many more.

128 pages   **$24.95**   **ISBN: 1-887432-86-8**

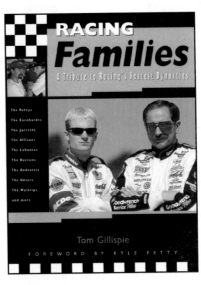

Racing Families:
A Tribute to Racing's Fastest Dynasties

NASCAR can certainly be considered a family tradition. The more than 50-year-old sport has been forged with strong family ties. And many racing family trees contain branches with three generations of drivers. In words and pictures, this book tells the story of the Pettys, the Allisons, the Jarretts, the Labontes, the Earnhardts and nine other families that are the lifeblood of NASCAR.

128 pages   **$24.95**   **ISBN: 1-887432-87-6**

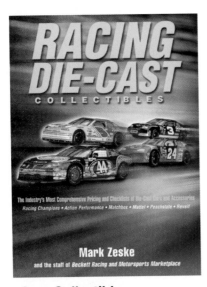

Racing Die-Cast Collectibles

This incredible book features page after page of color photos, pricing and checklists for all scales of racing die-cast cars. Manufacturers listed include Racing Champions, Action Performance, Revell, Winner's Circle, Hot Wheels and many more. Includes sections on how to start your collection and hints for storage and display, plus checklists for the top 12 NASCAR drivers.

256 pages   **$24.95**   **ISBN: 1-887432-81-7**

Beckett Racing Collectibles
and Die-Cast Price Guide No. 5

New edition! Now with the most comprehensive coverage of die-cast cars available anywhere. Includes up-to-date die-cast pricing, plus prices and alphabetical driver listings for every racing card ever issued. Covers NASCAR, IndyCar, Formula One, NHRA, Sprint Cars and more. Over 1,000 card set listings and 6,000 die-cast replica listings.

496 pages   **$14.95**   **ISBN:1-887432-91-4**